Plutonic Sonnets

By

Robert Bates Graber

PublishAmerica
Baltimore

© 2008 by Robert Bates Graber.
All rights reserved. No part of this book may be reproduced, stored in a retrieval system or transmitted in any form or by any means without the prior written permission of the publishers, except by a reviewer who may quote brief passages in a review to be printed in a newspaper, magazine or journal.

First printing

PublishAmerica has allowed this work to remain exactly as the author intended, verbatim, without editorial input.

ISBN: 1-60703-224-4
PUBLISHED BY PUBLISHAMERICA, LLLP
www.publishamerica.com
Baltimore

Printed in the United States of America

*To the memory of Elizabeth Graeme Fergusson
in lasting gratitude
to the poets of poetbay.com
and neopoet.com
for comments on drafts of the sonnets*

THE SONNETS

I

(To Samos)

Bright gem of the Aegean! Who will dare
To ope' the treasure thou hast giv'n our kind,
To take its measure, so beyond compare,
And tell what thou hast meant for human mind?
Pythagoras himself was thine own son,
Whose harmonies across the ages ring;
And clear-eyed Epicurus was the one
Who stared down death itself, and dulled its sting.
And tow'ring Aristarchus: it was he
Who placed among the planets his own world
By recognizing that the Sun must be
The center 'round which we and they all whirled.
Fair-crested isle! Can glowing sun e'er kiss,
On any world, a nobler peak than this?

II

(To Aristarchus)

Lucretius indeed in very Rome
Brought Epicurus back to vibrant life;
And Shakespeare was by London lured from home,
To lift that crowded heart of madding strife.
Yet the great Kant from his accustomed course
'Round little Königsberg nothing could tease:
'Twas there he sought morality's true source;
From there in thought he soared to galaxies.
And had not your fair Samos come to be
On edge of Persian or Athenian power,
Where vain conceits of self-centrality
Through absence brought your genius to flower?
For flowers blossom out in petaled rings,
And butterflies bear glory in their wings!

III

(To Democritus)

"Nothing exists but atoms and the void."
The bravery to utter words like these
By Athens was so utterly destroyed,
You dared not show your face to Socrates.
You cared but little for the world's applause,
But much for circle, cylinder, and cone;
You said you'd rather understand one cause
Than occupy the King of Persia's throne.
Your universe of particles, finite
In kind but recombined in endless ways,
Would wait two thousand years to shed such light
As raised it to the throne on which it stays;
In darkness lies the Sun King, long congealed,
While in your light the Cosmos stands revealed!

IV

For gods the Romans named the wand'ring stars;
But five could they, like those before them, see.
To honor war, they called the red one Mars;
The speedy one, was it not Mercury,
Swift messenger by whom gods' words took wing?
A bright and stately traveler sublime
They christened Jupiter, the gods' own king.
The slowest they called Saturn, god of time;
The brightest, fair Venus, goddess of love.
And two great bodies more, the Moon and Sun,
That roam by night and day the heav'ns above,
Round out the sev'n, of which Earth was not one.
Homebody she, no rover of the skies!
And still as Aristarchus's surmise.

V

The cycle of light and dark defines our days,
And changing seasons demarcate our years;
Our months reflect the course of lunar phase;
Yet no such solid base for weeks appears!
The ancients, gazing up, saw two great lights,
And wand'ring stars but five. We need not seek
A source beyond these seven wondrous sights
For seven days and nights being one week.
Thus Satur(n)day, Sunday, Mo(o)nday make sense
(In Romance languages the link's most clear).
And seven are the Christian sacraments,
As are the deadly sins the faithful fear;
And alch'my's shiny metals numbered seven—
Substantially on Earth as 'twas in heaven.

VI

Now droops the raven slouched upon a skull—
Saturn is lead: the Black Work is begun!
The bird's slow rot it sees with eyes now dull;
And Jupiter is tin: the Black Work's done.
Two white birds on the remnant filth swoop down;
And Mars is iron: see the pair ascend,
Now bearing, far from Earth, the five-spiked crown!
The Sun is gold: the White Work's at an end.
O'er myst'ry egg the nesting pair now flies;
Venus is copper: the Red Work begins.
A unicorn before a rosebush lies;
Yes, Mercury is mercury: it grins.
A youthful androgyne steps from a grave;
The Moon is silver: What remains to save?

VII

O Marduk (Jupiter), 'tis in your grip,
And for your ease, we toil just to eat.
Fair Ishtar (Venus), did your sister strip
You, then turn you into a slab of meat?
And could the seven-headed snake e'en flee
Your stroke? Ninurta (Saturn), guard us, please!
Wise dragon-rider Nabu (Mercury),
Be gen'rous as you write our destinies!
Dread lion-headed Nergal (Mars), so feared:
Have mercy, lord of wars and pestilence!
And Sin (Moon) on your bull, with your blue beard:
Our wise men chart your changes to make sense
Of our travail in this prevailing night;
O Shamash (Sun), disperse it with your light!

VIII

(To Ptolemy)

Mapmaker, we know nothing of your looks,
But quite a lot about the work you did.
Geographia, one of your great books,
A largely-unknown world trapped in a grid.
With spheres in spheres in spheres your *Almagest*
Sufficed for navigators of your day
While leaving Earth, the cosmic core, at rest.
Untrue? Your truth was spiritual, some say!
And *Tetrabiblos* tells us how the stars,
Not by themselves but rather in concert
With causes nearer than the Moon or Mars,
Our natures and our projects help or hurt.
And folks in shacks and mansions still hold on
To lore you culled from ancient Babylon.

IX

So what's your sign? Aquarius you say?
The Water-Bearer! Oh, you must be bright,
A believer in pure reason, clear as day.
Shall we pair up forever? For tonight?
Forgive me. Did you know that Uranus
Your ruler planet is? It takes the part
(Just *entre nous* [between the two of us])
Of intuition—thinking with the heart.
And so the best astrologers agree:
In light of the dual nature of your sign,
The coming age is predestined to see
Your reason and my faith sweetly combine.
In short, our match is made in heav'n above;
Now is the dawning of the Age of Love!

X

Did not what we call Earth go 'round the Sun,
And sweep her own elliptic pathway clean,
Long, long before she hosted anyone
To talk about what "planet" ought to mean?
Was not that body relatively round,
And large as well, before thereon was heard,
By female frog, a plaintive croak resound,
And long before our kind's first halting word?
In gen'ral, words don't *make* what they're about,
But make *sense of it*—still a lot to ask;
We redefine them as we figure out
What they should mean, to better do this task.
As planets must along their course revolve,
Our definitions cannot but evolve!

XI

In the beginning God made heav'n and Earth.
"Let there be light," God said; and there was light.
And not as light alone did lights have worth,
For they marked years and seasons, day from night.
And made he also all things here below,
And this must be distinctly understood:
From scripture we are privileged to know
That God, when he was done, saw *all* was good.
And Eden for a time was perfect too,
'Til the first couple, in God's image made,
Corrupted all things earthly, through and through,
When, tempted by the snake, they disobeyed.
"But in the heav'ns," their tainted seed would sigh,
"'Tis ours, divine perfection to espy!"

XII

Was Evil made by Adam and by Eve?
If so, who gave them this propensity
If not their Maker? Herein we perceive
A thorny problem of theology.
Some say God gave us freedom of the will,
From which, as in the Garden, evils fall.
But why not make us to choose good, not ill?
(And Nature plagues us from no choice at all.)
"The highest Good's when Evil's overcome,"
Some say; and for this, Evil there must be.
But can such need explain its awful sum?
It often seems to gain the victory!
The problem stands. Shall we bid it good-bye,
Or tarry long enough for one more try?

XIII

At the outset, did God, who all things knew,
Consider all the worlds that could be,
And then create the best that he could do
Within the realm of possibility?
Though of some pow'r this seems God to divest,
So Leibniz said; but with its endless woes
Our world reduces this to bitter jest,
As Pangloss of Voltaire's *Candide* well shows.
May it not be that "Good" is just the word
We give to what is noblest in our eyes?
And "Evil" just the English term preferred
For everything we utterly despise?
Such sentiments we scarcely can but feel…
Enough. With the rest, those who will may deal.

XIV

What's harder to believe than that Earth moves?
Most of the time it stands completely still,
As common sense experience daily proves;
Denying this still takes an act of will!
And once attained, the belief's not eas'ly kept:
For eighteen hundred years the great surmise
Of Aristarchus, quite forgotten, slept
Through many a so-called sunset and sunrise.
Now, since such terms are biblically correct,
Both church and common sense by Nicholas
Copernicus were ired; friends, to protect
Him, offered, 'gainst this allied animus:
"Though his strange system's better for prediction,
He sees it only as a useful fiction"!

XV

(To Giordano Bruno)

Unpopular beliefs o'erflow your mind,
Giordano Bruno. Few will know your name;
You aren't too rare for us to know your kind!
You are the flitting moth drawn to the flame.
You write of endless worlds without end,
Yet won't allow that God is even three;
You've made, then driv'n away, more than one friend
With your foul river of rank heresy.
You spew false teachings on our holy Mass,
And practice magic! We cannot but see
Your views on Christ as unspeakably crass;
To Mary you deny virginity!
'Tis more than Christianity can take;
'Tis for these crimes we burn you at the stake.

XVI

(To Tycho Brahe)

How stupid could you be? Enough to fight
A duel o'er who was best at math, we're told;
And therein lose your nose, which wasn't bright,
Until you got a new one made of gold!
How petty could you be? Enough to toy
With stern young Kepler when he stood in need
Of data. Was it that he took no joy
In the rich-playboy life he saw you lead?
And yet, in nights before the telescope,
You were an awesome watcher of the sky;
Your records were germane to Kepler's hope
To find the rules by which the planets fly.
You needed him as well, as well you knew;
Your legacy depended on his brain,
Which you enlisted when your life was through:
—"Let me not seem to have lived in vain!"

XVII

Pythagoras five perfect solids knew,
With faces numb'ring four or six (the cube)
Or eight or twelve or twenty; that these few
Are all that there can be, even a rube
Such as Johannes Kepler was aware.
Math teacher and Copernican was he;
And one day, as he taught, in moment rare
Was giv'n to him the Cosmic Mystery:
Six orbits round [O] for six planets, defined
By nested solids five [P]—purely not geo-
But heliocentric was the Maker's mind:
O-P-O-P-O-P-O-P-O-P-O !
But Tycho's work said no, and Kepler found
The Myst'ry false; orbits, not even round.

XVIII

Could God have made the orbits less than round?
The thought appeared to Kepler far from pious;
A load of dung, he cried, was all he'd found!
Yet thus he overcame an ancient bias:
If Earth, of lowly stuff, and to such reek
Can be the home, and still a planet be,
In other planets, or their paths, why seek
Perfection—as we see it—there to see?
To th' ellipse Kepler found a perfect fit,
And also two more laws would formulate;
The last was seed, as Newton did admit,
Of his great law of how things gravitate.
Rich harvest have we had from Kepler's toil:
Sweet fruit indeed has grown from fertile soil!

XIX

So just why is there anything at all,
Instead of mere eternal nothingness?
Now there's a question that may seem to call
For trenchant philosophical address!
Well, what about that primeval Big Bang?
From there our Universe *appears* to flow;
And if *indeed* from there the Cosmos sprang,
Has science told us what we want to know?
Here's one objection worth reflecting on:
That bang, although it may have set in train
All else, itself, as a phenomenon,
Is part of what we're trying to explain!
So science has its limits. Is it odd
That some see this as evidence of God?

XX

From Descartes' *cogito* we know he found
His body he could doubt, but not his mind;
And Gassendi, for deeming this unsound,
Descartes called carnal—scarcely fair or kind.
And no great courage did Descartes display
When he reported having come to see
That he had been abjectly wrong to say
Earth moved. He loved divine authority!
And this abrupt reversal to excuse,
Declared, "To live well you must live unseen."
Thus did a believer in pure mind misuse
What Epicurus said, to make it mean
What Epicurus never would have claimed:
That hypocrites may well feel unashamed.

XXI

For Epicurus Descartes had no time,
So far from a materialist was he;
Until he, so to speak, turned on a dime,
And Earth no longer turned, he now could see!
And Epicurus suddenly was wise
In praising life outside the spotlight's glare—
A most convenient way to moralize
Capitulating to canonic blare.
I would in private he had thought or said,
"Earth moves, and it's a fact one might well vie for;
But frankly, Bruno's end fills me with dread;
'Tis not a fact to suffer or to die for!"
Capitulation, in itself quite sensible,
Wrapped in false virtue's downright reprehensible.

XXII

Vincenzo Galilei played the lute
And studied it experimentally.
At composition, too, he was astute;
He married late, into nobility.
Though busy and already on in years,
Time with his sev'ral children he would take;
One—Michaelagnolo—displayed keen ears
And fingers; he a lutenist would make.
Another of the children's minds found wings
While helping or just watching, eyes aglow,
His father fussing with vibrating strings,
And using math to liven up the show.
Vincenzo's lute into the Cosmos grew,
Ere Galileo—his firstborn—was through!

XXIII

Was Galileo bright and handy too?
Indeed! The telescope, when he was done,
Was ten times stronger, and much more could do,
Than the Dutch spyglass with which he'd begun.
Some fancy gadgets Tycho had employed
For charting stars, but only naked eyes
For looking at them; what an edge enjoyed
The now-prosthetic watcher of the skies!
Four shifting dots near Jupiter aligned
Was Galileo thus allowed to see.
(The names he gave were prudently assigned
To honor his patrons, the Medici.)
For heliocentrism, this had subtle worth:
Orbs wheeling 'round a hub that was not Earth!

XXIV

To glorify his famous patrons' name,
"The Medicean Planets, One through Four"
His new stars Galileo dubbed. How lame!
Are not these monikers a cosmic bore?
Now Simon Marius, who claimed he'd viewed
The new stars first, heard Kepler was quite keen
On names that would to Jupiter allude,
And thus would be, one might say, less routine.
Though Simon's claim did not hold up, he seemed
To glimpse that merely naming stars might be
Some claim to fame (even if never deemed
A subject suitable for sonnetry).
And Galileo's dull names long held sway,
But Simon's bright ones finally won the day.

XXV

To hide her from wife Juno's prying eyes,
Of *Io* Jupiter a heifer made;
Astride a swimming bull on ocean's rise,
Europa rode with him, but grew afraid.
And Jupiter, as eagle, took to th' air
With *Ganymede*, the handsome Trojan boy,
And took him all the way to heaven, where
The gods could him as cup-bearer enjoy.
And of *Callisto* Juno made a bear,
But bear too gentle in the wilds to stay;
So Jupiter raised her aloft, up where
She stays, as Ursa Minor, to this day.
Is it not nice, and not a little funny,
That antics of the gods trumped patron's money?

XXVI

(To Marina Gamba)

Was it with gladness or with some regret
You left your native Venice and went west
To move in with your boyfriend and beget
Three children in your Paduan love-nest?
The first was bright Virginia, born the year
By church your lover loved was Bruno burned;
The next was Livia, sickly, quiet, queer;
Vincenzio was last. No one has learned,
When growing fame and fortune took your beau
To Florence with his girls in 1610,
Just why it was you let each other go;
Or why in 1613, the year when
Your daughters' cloistered sisters' lives began,
You finally married—another man.

XXVII

(To Galileo Galilei)

You with your live-in lover children had,
In what your church then called, and still calls, sin;
They say your household life was far from bad,
Except for when your mother butted in...
And yet you left; and with you when you went
Were your two girls of only nine or ten,
Who to a nunn'ry soon by you were sent.
(Your boy of four stayed with his mother then.)
Well, Galileo, I have heard you loved
Your church and children too, which I don't doubt;
But at first blush, it looks as if you shoved
Your children from you, and dared to flout
Your church. So if you truly held them dear,
The bare facts of your life don't make it clear.

XXVIII

When Bruno had been tried for heresy,
Instead of answering with easy lie,
His judges he had challenged openly
As more afraid to damn than he to die.
His burning proved their readiness to kill,
So Galileo knew they played no games:
When they said he must say the Earth stood still,
He said it, rather than go up in flames;
And yet, so deep their ignorance and fear,
His last eight years lived under house arrest.
But whether at the time, too soft to hear,
Or only later, thus did he attest:
"E pur si muove"—*and yet it moves!*
So much for what a forced confession proves.

XXIX

(To Maria Celeste)

You must have been the apple of his eye;
I like to think, Virginia, that you were
His little helper too, and did espy,
That winter's night, the moons of Jupiter.
You seem by no means to have thought him mean,
To judge by the new name you soon would fashion,
When he convented you at age thirteen:
It honored Mary, and your father's passion!
By medicines and letters was he blest
'Til dysentery ended your brief race;
But not ere you, alongside whom he'd rest,
Had lived to suffer with him his disgrace.
So did the church they loved repay with woe
Virginia Gamba and Galileo.

XXX

(To Christiaan Huygens)

Imaginer of worlds, you claimed this world
Your only nation was; and for your creed
Science alone! As Holland's ships unfurled
Their sails, just so, her finest minds were freed.
Where even common folks believed Earth moved,
Your genius was duly celebrated,
When elsewhere you'd have likely been reproved
Or tortured, and perhaps incinerated.
You even wrote the first book on the odds,
And found a moon of Saturn and baptized
It *Titan*, for the parents of the gods.
Th' Orion Nebula you analyzed,
Where nameless, dateless stars are born and shine:
Hail Christiaan Huygens, 1629!

XXXI

The center of the Hunter's blade's not keen,
And it's a bit of a curiosity
That by great Galileo was not seen
Its rather distinct nebulosity.
Now we can see it, but can't see it *now*:
Its light has taken fifteen hundred years
To reach remote prostheses that allow
Us in on sunbirth. It now appears
That crests and cavities light-years in size
By winds from four huge stars are being blown,
While lesser clouds collapse and new suns rise
Amidst organic matter to us known
From burning toast and tail pipes of our cars—
Strange swaddling of a thousand infant stars!

XXXII

The Goldilocks Zone! Not too hot or cold,
Where water as a liquid can flow free:
'Til now this rare condition seemed to hold
On Earth alone, as far as we could see.
But now, five times more massive than our own,
A distant world around a distant sun,
With temperatures in Goldilocks' rare zone,
Once every thirteen days appears to run.
Compared to suns like ours, red dwarves are cool,
So "Gliese Five Eighty-One" holds Goldie close;
But Sasselov of Harvard, no one's fool,
Is likely being less than grandiose
When he says this red dwarf may have to share:
"It's twenty light-years—we can go there!"

XXXIII

With Earth no more the point of reference,
But just another planet out of six,
A cosmic stress on seven made no sense,
And numerology needed a fix.
So six, as not devoid of mystery,
Was taken, duly dusted, from the shelf;
Did its divisors, one and two and three,
Not add up to exactly six itself?
Six planets and six moons would have been fine,
But Galileo's Medicean four
Plus ours made five, too few to seem divine;
If only there could be just one moon more…
Then enter Titan! No one needed seven,
Once Huygens had restored God to his heaven!

XXXIV

Six planets and six moons: a package neat
By Titan tightened and so snugly bound
That even Huygens thought it was complete;
Why look for more when no more would be found?
But an observatory soon would rise
In Paris, where the Sun King had discerned
The man most likely to immortalize
Him was Cassini, so to him he turned.
Thus Giovanni Domenico soon
"Jean-Dominique" became, and caught a wave
When swam into his ken not one new moon
Of Saturn, but two, which he proudly "gave"
To Louis, to whose pleasure 'twas now seen
Not twelve the heavens honored, but fourteen!

XXXV

(To Hennig Brand)

From soldiering you turned to alchemy;
To make gold from base matter was your dream.
And did your first wife watch contentedly
As you squandered her fortune on this scheme?
She died, and so another wife you found,
And by good fortune, she'd a fortune too;
So though you never *made* gold, from the sound
Of things, for *digging* it your touch was true!
Of urine by the bucket you made use;
(Draw gold from gold: Did thus your thinking go?)
But all your secret process would produce
Was funny stuff that gave a pale-green glow.
For finding phosphorus you're given credit;
'Tis more than you deserve! There, I've said it.

XXXVI

In France was quick Cassini quick to find
A Saturn moon he named Iapetus
(The Titan called the father of mankind,
And sire of Atlas and Prometheus).
A second he named Rhea, for the mother
Of Zeus and all the gods; due to the math
He then stopped looking, lest he find another—
A fifteenth, and incur a XIV's wrath!
But after twelve years he could stand no more;
And sighted Tethys, named for Titan who
Three thousand children her own brother bore,
And Dione (moth'r of Aphrodite) too;
Then, noting Galileo'd done the same,
Gave all four moons, *en masse*, his patron's name.

XXXVII

(To Jean-Dominique Cassini)

Cassini, brains like yours one seldom sees:
Recruited, not yet twenty, to turn pro,
And labor to improve astrology's
Suppos'd pow'r to predict things here below.
And this called for close study of the skies,
A project that engrossed you more and more;
Were not some colleagues wont to criticize
You for forgetting what it was all for?
Wooed by the Pope to be his engineer,
You chose to stay the Sun King's star of stars,
Lest practical endeavors interfere
With working out how far it was to Mars!
And so a science of the heavens grew
Just for itself, not for what it could do.

XXXVIII

(To Isaac Newton)

A pebble: it is difficult to name
An object more conveniently discrete;
Yet "calculus" (or 'pebble') somehow came
To name the branch of math with which we treat
All nature's deepest continuities.
Can any human thing be more sublime
Than this, the key unlocking mysteries
Of variation over space and time?
Oh shingle-minded boy searching the shore,
What gems you found! The calculus of course;
And that the apple falling t'ward Earth's core
Is drawn, and drawn there by the very force
By which the breakers to the beach are curled,
And planets 'round their mighty suns are hurled.

XXXIX

The area of a rectangle is base
Times height, and as day rises from the night,
It follows, from this lowly starting place,
Dividing area by the base gives height.
Therefore an area 'neath a function's curve
(To keep all things from falling out of joint)
Divided by a shrinking base must serve
To near the function's value at a point.
To many students, sharp in other ways,
How dull a disappearing act this seems!
Unlit by Leibniz are their college days,
And darkened by great Newton are their dreams.
And yet these very ever-closing bars
Have opened wide a gateway to the stars.

XL

When barriers to our love filled my poor head
With clouds of fear I feared I could not ban,
She came to me and oh so softly said,
"Let's just enjoy each other while we can."
At that the Sun came streaming through the gloom;
And in its light I heard our dear Earth say,
"Enjoy me, but do not too far presume,
Or with its very life your kind will pay."
In darkness came the Cosmos, while I dreamed
(Amazing it should pay us any mind!),
And coyly admitted (so it seemed),
"Yours really is a somewhat special kind."
Then sweet it came to me: my answer ran,
"Let's just enjoy each other while we can."

XLI

The sky god, born of Earth, engorged her womb
With babies he declared he'd kill if born.
Sad Gaia! Would her belly be their tomb,
Or would she see them slaughtered ere she mourn?
She held them in 'til she could bear no more,
'Til tightened womb indeed was so distended
That out they popped! And thus in fear she bore
The race from which our race would be descended.
But wait! Was not this god-forsaken brood
Born but to die at Uranus's hand?
Not so: the lastborn's angry stroke, though crude,
Was fell, and he his own old man unmanned;
And so it was that Saturn, with his sickle,
Freed father and his seed from godly pickle!

XLII

(To John Flamsteed)

They say your brewer father could not see
Just what on Earth your hobby could be for;
Yet in your youth your king called you to be
His Astronomical Observator.
And Tycho, whom you called "the noble Dane,"
Inspired you to chart the stars that clad
The night; your catalogue would greatly gain
From new tools and techniques he had not had.
Newton and Halley, earthly stars indeed,
Found you too slow your duty to fulfill
To king and colleagues; but did they need
To publish your star book against your will?
Most copies you proceeded to acquire
And burn, in protest, in a public fire!

XLIII

(To Uranus)

A half a dozen times ere he was through
John Flamsteed saw you, but not what you are.
A dozen times Le Monnier saw you too;
And he, like Flamsteed, took you for a star.
Next Herschel, who was first to see you *move*,
You fooled as to your status up in heaven:
He called you comet—though you'd soon prove
No comet, but our system's planet seven!
The planets had already all been found:
So all had thought; since no more of that kind
Were thought to be, their thought was thus far bound;
And thought thus bounded made them thus far blind.
So let's remind ourselves to look for more
Than what it is we think we're looking for.

XLIV

Coordinates are a good way to show
Above as well as on the Earth, what's where;
And what's called longitude for what's below,
Is "right ascension" when the "what"'s up there.
In Flamsteed's early work, which Newton copped,
Was this, plus constellation's name, applied
To name a star—a system Flamsteed dropped
Ere he with his own book was satisfied.
Most of the old books, Flamsteed set aflame;
But their star-naming system would not die.
(Though one "star" that would merit a new name,
As planet, was old "34 tauri"!)
The best of something that someone has done
Sometimes is seen best by some other one.

XLV

One of ten children born to German Jew
And Christian wife, an Englishman became;
Musician was he, 'til age forty-two,
When he achieved a different kind of fame.
His music's faded long into the past,
But March 13, 1781,
Herschel became both first and next-to-last
Discov'rer of a planet 'round our Sun.
He had a speculative turn of mind
That did not always serve him very well;
Would you believe he even once opined
That big-brained beings on the Sun must dwell?
So put it down as a good rule of thumb:
The smartest people can be really dumb!

XLVI

The moving object William Herschel found
No comet shortly proved itself to be;
Its orbit was for that too nearly round,
As Herschel and Laplace soon came to see.
And shall we say our Sun a planet gained?
Or had a planet been there all along?
The latter! Lest we find ourselves constrained
From saying calling it a star'd been *wrong*!
To call a thing a certain thing is not
To make it that; and neither can it call
Into existence e'en the tiniest jot,
And thus make something from nothing at all!
Was finding it like reading Chapman's Homer?
Perhaps; but "George's Star" proved a misnomer.

XLVII

By naming the new planet for his king
(Viz. "George's Star," in Latin, *Georgium Sidus*),
Will Herschel did for Herschel no bad thing:
He turned his find to gold, like good old Midas!
When nits were picked about what *sidus* meant,
This label proved by no means carved in granite:
The king's new star was happy to relent,
And quickly changed the name to George's *Planet*.
But outside Britain, this was still a bust;
Indeed, the planet's name caused grave dissension.
The French rejected it, and no doubt cussed
It for retaining British monarch's mention.
Like Galileo and Cassini, Herschel
Could pick a name from motives quite commercial.

XLVIII

(To Elizabeth Graeme Fergusson)

Ben Franklin's bastard was to be your groom,
But somehow (I don't really know the story)
Instead, in your mid-thirties you'd assume
The name of H. H. Fergusson, a Tory.
Your elegance and wit made you the toast
Of Philadelphia, from where the sting
Of your sharp pen reached England's very coast,
To mock the failures of a fading king.
"A star is found, that's clear," you wrote, "and hail'd"
(By Herschel) with the British monarch's name;
You ended, "If terrestrial glory's failed,"
It mattered not: "The Heavens enroll his fame."
You kept, though not your husband, your Graeme Park;
And left me this bright candle in the dark:

IL

Upon the Discovery of the Planet By Mr. Herschel of Bath and By Him Nam'd the Georgium Sidus in Honor of his Britannic Majesty (By Elizabeth Graeme Fergusson, c. 1781)

Whether the optic's piercing eyes
Have introduced to view
A distant planet of the skies,
Bright, wonderful, and new?
Or whether we are nearer thrown
To the grand fount of light,
And from that source each mist is flown
That wrapt the star in night?
Too deep this point, a female pen
Dare not such heights explore;
The subject's left to learned men
Of philosophic lore!
A star is found, that's clear, and hail'd
With Britain's monarch's name;
If terrestrial glory's fail'd,
The Heavens enroll his fame.

L

The heavens would not long enroll the fame
Of George the Third, that unsuccessful king:
By 1850, the new planet's name
That flattered him was an outmoded thing.
Now, Mars was godly son of Jupiter;
And Jupiter, in turn, was Saturn's son.
How hard is it, from these facts, to infer
The *proper* name to carry on this run?
So thought the winking German, Johann Bode
(Though Saturn's father wasn't very nice:
His children he'd have slain, the rotten toad,
Had Saturn not fixed *him* with well-aimed slice!).
And mytho-logic won: the naming fuss
Came to a fitting end with "Uranus."

LI

(To Johann Elert Bode)

One of your eyelids drooped, as if to wink,
And yet the law you wrote saw very far;
'Twas not in jest, and people came to think
It ruled how planets ranged around their star.
And better yet it looked when Herschel found
A planet new (which you named perfectly
As Uranus), because it traveled 'round
The Sun just where your law said it should be!
But did you not roll over in your grave,
When Neptune's orbit sank your law so low?
Nay, patience! It may rise on a new wave
When other systems we have come to know!
You'll roll back over then, I like to think,
And maybe rouse yourself to throw a wink.

LII

Twelve meters long was Herschel's largest scope;
That's forty feet, and it was four feet wide.
And I am sure it was with highest hope
This monster he against the darkness tried.
And sure enough, unearthed on its first night
Was a new moon of Saturn; and one more
Soon followed, so its future sparkled bright.
What new sky-buried treasures lay in store?
And yet a telescope just half this size
Most useful to Will Herschel was to prove.
Perhaps it ought to come as no surprise;
The larger one was just too hard to move!
For moral here we need not deeply dig:
We do well not to worship all that's big.

LIII

They say four hundred telescopes were "built
By William Herschel," and I'm sure it's true
He supervised; but is there not some guilt
In giving to the great more than their due?
His forty-foot behemoth—See here!
The carpenters who built its sturdy frame,
The foundry men who poured its four-foot mirror:
Did not each have a story and a name?
I have no wish to sound like saint or priest
Or much to sermonize on what is sin;
But those behind the "great": Could we at least
Not speak as if they had not even *been*?
For ruler never raised a temple high,
And I will not say "Louis built Versailles."

LIV

(To Caroline Lucretia Herschel)

You were eleven years younger than he;
You sang his music, and you sang it well;
And when he shifted to astronomy,
You shifted with him, and would soon excel.
Your compact scope, untiring, swept the sky;
At least five comets you were first to view,
In light of which it's easy to see why
King George the Third put you on sal'ry too.
At nearly fifty, Will first took a wife,
And you moved out, but not of your alliance:
You helped him 'til his end. You gave your life
Of ninety-seven years to him and science.
Could anyone a higher service render
Than you, who showed that knowing knows no gender?

LV

When a new planet came within his scope,
The good Brit Herschel dubbed it "George's Star."
Mars, Jupiter, and Saturn: Need one grope?
No name but "Uranus" was up to par!
It is the patriline of Roman gods,
As Bode in Germany was quick to see.
But slowly, slowly reason often plods;
It took the world some decades to agree.
But German chemist Klaproth liked the name;
And, helped by methods learned from Lavoisier,
Discovered a new element the same
Year France broke out in its colossal fray.
Let revolutions make whole nations quake;
Uranium the Earth itself would shake.

LVI

(To Antoine Lavoisier)

Of just exactly what do things consist?
So deep the order you so deeply sought!
Of "simple substances" you made a list,
And wrote the first book from which chemists taught.
Though several on your list of thirty-three,
Like "heat" and "light," we find ourselves unable
To countenance, with two-thirds we agree
So well they're in our own periodic table.
You'd have seen more (how much we do not know),
But deep'ning social chaos closed your eyes;
When wild the winds of revolution blow,
They scorn to tell the vicious from the wise.
"France has no need of geniuses," they said;
And in their frenzy—cut off your head.

LVII

Earth, water, air, and fire: each had its home
To which things out of place tend to return;
And fire dwelt beyond the airy dome,
So where but *up* should earthly fires burn?
Around the wat'ry sphere's the airy ball,
So air bubbles in water have to rise;
And objects, being earth, to Earth must fall
(Which scarcely seems an ungrounded surmise).
The ancients' "wand'ring stars" turned out to be
Among our planets, but their elements
In our periodic table we don't see;
Eventually their science made no sense.
And yet when lightning strikes, I swear I love
To think it's fire leaking from above.

LVIII

(To Ceres [Ferdinandea])

The gap from Mars to Jupiter should hold
A planet, by Bode's Law, and sure enough:
Piazzi found you there! The world was told,
And you were hailed as planetary stuff.
But soon there proved to be a whole big belt
Of bodies out there circling 'round the Sun;
And when Bode's Law by Neptune soon was dealt
An awful blow, as planet you were done.
Though large enough to make yourself a ball,
And truly huge as asteroids go,
In planetary terms a "dwarf" is all
You are, and smallest of the three we know.
Yet o'er vast reaches still you reign supreme,
And Ferdinand's brief glory's but a dream.

LIX

(To John Dalton)

A Universe of atoms in the void:
Some Greeks had tried, but could not make it stick.
And it's a fact I often have enjoyed:
A sober English Quaker did the trick.
That gas was particles bouncing around
In space, some others had begun to say;
But liquids, even solids? Yes! You found
The model could be driven all the way.
The Bible says the blind shall see; the dumb
Shall sing in joy. Well, color-blind were you,
And inarticulate. Your life sounds glum:
You never married, and your friends were few.
Yet soaring thoughts bring joy, and you had ears
To hear the truth across two thousand years.

LX

(To Dmitri Mendeleev)

When you told Anna you'd take your own life
Unless she married you, was it an act?
Your method, though pathetic, worked: your wife
She soon became, despite one little fact
Which some folks thought was worthy of respect:
You *had* a wife, and had for fourteen years!
The Russian Academy declared, "Reject,"
Due to appearances, so it appears.
But you saw patterns no one else could see;
And if your private life was, well, unstable,
You wowed the world when you predicted three
New elements with your "periodic table."
And though it sounds like something of a spoof,
You are the reason vodka's 80 proof.

LXI

Sir William Herschel had a son named John
Who followed him into astronomy;
And names John gave to moons really caught on.
For Uranus he drew on poetry:
Sprites Ariel and Umbriel do play
Indeed in Pope's great *Rape*, and also scheme;
Titania and Oberon hold sway
To rule the fairy land of Shakespeare's *Dream*.
Of Saturn, seven satellites were known;
For Titans John made them eponymous:
Minas, Enceladus, Tethys, Dione,
And Rhea, Titan, and Iapetus.
('Round Saturn they do well to keep their path:
'Twas he who'd saved them from their father's wrath!)

LXII

A fine and comely couple, it appears,
The Herschels were, and they made babies fast:
They had eleven kids in sixteen years,
And then a twelfth when nine more years had passed.
"The mystery of mysteries" John phrased
The origin of species; Darwin solved
This mystery, and left the world amazed,
By showing how the living world evolved.
That many more are born than can survive,
To Darwin proved a most important clue;
For this meant Nature must, as beings strive,
"Select" the fit; What else could Nature do?
And life's prepotency to multiply,
The Herschels did themselves exemplify!

LXIII

To reach the very top! Some have to try
To scale the utmost height; for this they dare
To risk their lives and fortunes—and why?
Three words said Mallory: "Because it's there!"
And so to storied Everest in Nepal
The summit-seekers go; and though that tor
Is high, some say the highest peak of all
Is Chimborazo, down in Ecuador.
A bulging middle circumscribes our Earth
(And some of us); though Everest is the place
Highest above the sea, this central girth
Boosts Chimborazo further into space.
The mountain we should climb, 'tis plain to see,
Depends on where it is we want to be.

LXIV

Look, look before you leap! Let us not doubt
That this is splendid counsel, and that we
Too seldom heed it, only to find out
That impulse yet again brings misery.
This big brain balanced on our aching spine
Can scarcely be worth bearing, but to give
Us foresight into what lies down the line
If we do this or that, *that we might live*.
Yet stand we not, at times, on some high ledge
Where stretching only proves that we, to win
Our chance, must leap—or step back from the edge,
To weep forever for what might have been?
Perhaps. But we may also simply fall,
And die for what was never there at all.

LXV

The ground beneath our feet, it seems to me,
We often take for granted, but it's worth
A lot: it holds us up! Without it, we
Would plummet toward the center of the Earth.
To most of us I rather think it must
Be a surprise to learn, though it's correct,
That making up almost half of Earth's crust
Is oxygen. Is that what you'd expect?
Our airy element, down in the grime?
Indeed, and there to silicon it's bound,
In feldspar, four O atoms at a time;
Two at a time in quartz is how it's found.
And on these minerals we take our stand,
Be it on solid rock, or sinking sand.

LXVI

If parts, well weighed, still weigh less than a whole,
There must be something more to be teased out;
If finding a new element's your goal,
The value of this logic's beyond doubt.
And with it, Martin Heinrich Klaproth found
Uranium, and promptly named it for
The planet for which Herschel was renowned.
This busy chemist did a whole lot more
Of which I here can do no more than say,
He named an element for our own orb.
Remembered, we remember M. H. K.
Best if we this into our minds absorb:
Look deeper when things don't add up's a rule
To follow if we would not play the fool.

LXVII

The composition of the crust of Earth,
Unlikely as the subject of a sonnet,
May yet provoke a modicum of mirth,
If one composes well enough upon it
(As one is wont to do). First place must go
To oxygen, which makes up nearly fifty
Percent by weight; and twenty-five or so
Is silicon. But Nature then grows thrifty:
Aluminum adds eight; iron, five more.
That's eighty-eight per cent, with eighty-eight
Elements yet to go! The one named for
Our planet, on the list comes very late;
Though Klaproth for "tellurium" was zealous,
There's precious little of it here on Tellus.

LXVIII

Since everything that's heavier than lead
Has, as its very nature, to break down,
A doubt has taken over my poor head
That "element" for them's a proper noun.
Things known full well to thus deteriorate,
We call true elements? I'd scarcely say
This seems a fitting way to designate
The mere decaying products of decay!
Incessant changes and infirmities:
Are not our lives and very selves yet filled—
Nay, emptied!—quite enough by such as these?
We long for something firm on which to build!
So if it's planetary to be round,
Is it not *elemental* to be sound?

LXIX

The elements are numbered by their Z's
(And lest you at the outset be misled:
My rhyme scheme here requires, if you please,
That letter "Z" be uttered "zee," not "zed").
The protons by the nucleus contained
Of constant number are; Z gives their number.
But then we find by no means thus constrained
The *neutrons* that the nucleus encumber.
As a matter of fact, due to the latter,
With *isotopes* we deal; and we are able
To say about them, as a fact of matter,
That some are stable, others quite unstable.
To be called true, an element, I'd hope,
Would have at least *one* stable isotope!

LXX

If we decide we want stability
In elements that we would count as true,
We must lop off, as false, all those with Z
Greater than lead's, which stands at 82.
To this fell stroke we may well gladly pay
Respects, for it advances us quite far,
By way of what is called alpha decay,
T'ward how many true elements there are.
But atoms can decay in other ways;
Indeed, Z's 43 and 61
By so-called beta and gamma decays
Are rendered false. *Voila!* Our trimming's done.
One major alpha cut, and some fine tuning:
Exactly eighty thus survive the pruning.

LXXI

The thought has suddenly occurred to me
That readers there may be of such a mind
To wonder what real benefit there be
To them in reading sonnets of this kind.
I ask them to remember how it is,
When at a big reception or a ball,
Some guy into his seventeenth gin fizz
Is being an obnoxious know-it-all.
You shouldn't throw your drink into his face,
Or push the latter into the pâté;
You might get punched, or tossed out of the place.
I modestly propose another way:
The conversation, first, you deftly turn
To elements, then ask him to report
Their current number, like you'd like to learn;
And when he says a hundred-some you snort,
"Sure, if you want to count stuff that's *unstable*!"
Then swagger off, to hit the hors d'oeuvre table.

LXXII

Some elements for planets have been named:
"Uranium" for Uranus is clear,
And Neptune by "neptunium"'s acclaimed
(Though only trace amounts of it are here).
And elemental praises have been sung
Even of "dwarves" like Ceres, which lays claim
To "cerium"; for Pluto, lately stung,
"Plutonium" still carries on its name.
But where is "earthium"? Can it be true
That namers of the elements have spurned
Our planet? No. Element fifty-two,
Tellurium, saves us from being burned:
This metal's named for 'Earth' in Latin, "Tellus";
So we tellurians need not be jealous!

LXXIII

A global body called the I. A. U.
Did def'nitely a definition fix,
To last how long, who knows? But it went through
On August 24, 2006.
A *planet*, I dare say, we will agree,
Around the Sun in orbit must be found;
"Sufficient mass for its self-gravity"
It also needs, to make it "nearly round";
And one thing more there is: it really must
Have "cleared the neighborhood around its orbit."
We layfolk here the I. A. U. must trust
(It takes an expert fully to absorb it);
But since the planet concept is negotiable,
May I opine it sounds a bit unsociable?

LXXIV

John Dalton saw that simple ratios
Recurred when certain substances combined,
As if they were small particles, and those
Of one bound strictly with the other kind.
And thus, experimental evidence
At last was found for what, so long ago,
Materialists had argued made most sense,
But had not demonstrated to be so.
And Feynman said, if for posterity
He had to choose a single fact to leave
To ease their torturous recovery
Of knowledge lost, here's what they should receive:
All things, from gas to cabbages and kings,
Consist of very, *very* little things.

LXXV

"The elements, they number 92,
At least in nature," so we used to say:
A scientific fact we thought we knew.
Things seem less clear in light of our own day:
Neptunium checked in at 93,
And then plutonium at 94;
First made by us, they later proved to be
In "nature." Who can say there won't be more?
And of the many more already made,
But (otherwise) not found, let's bear in mind
That as more here and elsewhere is displayed
To us by us, we know not what we'll find.
And this I would that we would take to heart:
Of Nature's vastness, we ourselves are part.

LXXVI

How many planets should we say there are?
For sev'ral decades we'd been saying nine,
'Til progress finally had brought us far
Enough to see we needed a new line.
Now, for eleven there's a case, I know;
But this includes three "dwarves," and experts say
Their number (not their size) is like to grow;
We'd like a number stable, come what may.
So let *our* count leave them out of account,
And stand at eight! And if the time should come
When this too is eroded by the fount
Of knowledge, let *theirs* be a better sum,
As definitions evolve to enable
Distinguishing the stable from unstable.

LXXVII

The atoms of a single isotope
Must be about as like as things can be,
Though that's the kind of thing one cannot hope
To ever absolutely guarantee.
The planets, on the other hand, both here
And elsewhere seem surprisingly unique.
(Therefore to find one much like ours, I fear
We shall have very far indeed to seek.)
So "Ceres" names *a thing*, that's clear enough;
We know of nothing else that's much the same.
But "cerium" denotes *the kind of stuff*
That sparks my pocket lighter—to flame;
And likewise "Neptune"'s "N," as upper case,
Would in "neptunium" be out of place.

LXXVIII

(To Neptune)

When thanks to Jove the giants' time was through,
You took your place as ruler of the deep;
And with your trident stirred the awesome brew
To waking frenzy—or let it sleep.
Upon the waters, mighty horses drew
Your chariot, pure gold their flowing mane!
Sea monsters strange, of every ghastly hue,
Made gaping way for brazen-hoofèd train!
But when fair Amphitrite you would woo,
You chose instead a dolphin for your steed,
Your courtship suiting well, as swift and true:
For courtly suitor's craft, a ship indeed!
And when your prize was won, his prize would be
To swim among the stars eternally.

LXXIX

(To Olin Jueck Eggen)

Oh country boy, how did it come to pass
That it was you who brought to light of day
That it was a collapsing cloud of gas
That spread the spiral of our Milky Way?
That you were something of a joker's clear,
Since those who knew you oft' remark upon it;
You claimed the Austin Healey you held dear
Three carburettors held beneath its bonnet!
But when you called "life in the dark" your life,
I can't believe your words were all in fun:
A war time buddy's widow was your wife
But briefly; and then when your life was done,
What came to light bespoke pathetic capers:
—Stolen Neptune documents and papers.

LXXX

"That star's not on the map!" a young man cried
In the Observatory of Berlin;
To which Galle, at the telescope, replied,
"God, it is a big fellow!" with a grin.
And thus was sighted, rising from the sea
Of stars beyond, not Triton with his horn,
But a new planet, *in reality*;
'Tis such as this should make us less forlorn!
Not clinging, childlike, to such childish things
As visions of the gods, whom we have made,
And made more than they are: imaginings,
Mere mirror images to which we've prayed!
Let others' worthy words their fading mourn;
I would we were into adulthood born.

LXXXI

(To John Couch Adams)

Strange, quiet low-born boy: Who knew your pain?
Buts pains we know you took in calculating,
As a young genius, how to explain
Why Uranus's course was deviating.
If in our system's icy reaches (where
But little sun can reach) a planet hid,
A normal orbit it could so impair
As to make Uranus move as it did.
You tried to give the R. G. O. a nudge
By dropping off a note to G. B. Airy;
But the observatory did not budge,
When you ignored his interested query.
Your silence was an unexpected course;
And where's the genius to disclose *its* source?

LXXXII

(To George Biddell Airy)

One autumn day in 1845,
A small young man in coat of fading green
Left you a note hinting you should contrive
To seek a hidden planet never seen.
A busy bureaucrat, you may have felt
A real appointment would have been better;
Or, barring that, might he at least have left
A somewhat longer and less cryptic letter?
Your letter in reply was quite polite,
But not exactly congratulatory;
If John Couch Adams took it as a slight,
That would explain the next part of the story:
Two pages were his letter's full extent,
A letter never finished, never sent.

LXXXIII

(To James Challis)

To hunt a planet you were far from keen,
When in October, 1845,
Young John Couch Adams said one had been seen
By him from his equations to derive.
But when, in June of 1846,
A paper by a Frenchman spelled things out,
The hunt was on, though you were in a fix,
With handicap you did not know about.
For months you toiled, star-mapping as you went
(I wonder how you found time for a nap);
While in Berlin, on the same game intent,
The Germans had a preexisting map!
They beat you only barely to the kill;
But theirs, the trophy; yours, a bitter pill.

LXXXIV

(To Urbain Le Verrier)

Astronomy in France had sunk quite low,
Long gone the great Cassini's glory days;
But you revitalized it, even though
Some chafed at your harsh manner and harsh ways.
You feared the march of secularity,
And found the hand of God in your research;
Your faith you put out front for all to see,
And bowed before the Holy Roman church.
Though I can't claim to be your greatest fan,
François Arago's tribute rings down through
The years, and in my ears, for that great man
Immortalized you as the mortal who
Discovered, *ere* it swam into our ken,
A planet with the point of a pen.

LXXXV

Le Verrier told the Germans where to aim
Their telescope to find a planet new;
Arago, ever keen, was keen to name
It for the one who'd told them what to do.
Though glasses clinked (*tchin-tchin!*) to this in France,
The Brits were loyal to their John Couch Adams;
The concept, frankly, stood but little chance
With people other than messieurs and madams.
Had Le Verrier himself not saved the day,
There may have frothed an ugly head of malice;
But in the 'stablished Roman-godly way,
He floated "Neptune," toasted well by Challis!
In all the years since all these things were done,
Neptune has not gone once around the Sun.

LXXXVI

With astronomical egg on their face,
The British did not hesitate to tout
The very Adams who, before the race,
They seem to have regarded with some doubt!
For long, their claim seemed better far than myth,
To the extent that hist'ry came to say
That Adams shared a glory equal with
The great Urbain Jean Joseph Le Verrier.
But when strange Eggen died, among his loot
Was Adams' note to Airy—quite meager;
And hero-seekers now their horns to toot
For Le Verrier alone seem very eager.
But Adams goes to show things had come 'round
For that which we call Neptune to be found.

LXXXVII

My love is lover of a planet blue,
Or images thereof; and I concede
That Neptune, seen from space, is of a hue
One might consider beautiful indeed.
But what's beneath that lovely atmosphere?
A barren, icy rock, so far from light
Of Sun, the Sun itself would there appear
As one among the stars in endless night.
I need not be so distant from *my* Sun
As Neptune, to be blue; but can you see?
Below's no darkling world of ice, but one
Warm-washed in endless light! How can this be?
'Tis that however far we are apart,
My love is with me, glowing in my heart.

LXXXVIII

Now to my winter comes a discontent,
When many whom I love are of a mind
To mark the birth of one they think was sent
To die, though sinless, for their sinful kind.
Their god of love demanded blood, you see;
The blood of his own son, whose life, in "fact,"
Was blameless. Their god does not seem to be
A being with whom I can make contact.
But as our planet courses 'round the Sun,
There comes a moment when, the moment passed,
Well blesses them, and me, and everyone
Whom Earth above her equator holds fast.
"Let there be light," we need no god to say;
We shall have less of night, and more of day!

LXXXIX

(To Walter Russell)

They seem to most of us less than your art,
Your cosmic views on mind and time and space;
And most parts, and the whole, for the most part
Fit poorly into scientific place.
Your strange periodic table had a twist,
A spiral in one sense more than nonsense;
The point has not been altogether missed:
It called for transuranic elements!
Great Mendeleev such predictions made;
Le Verrier and Couch Adams—their story
From hist'ry's pages is not like to fade;
But where for *you* the credit? Where the glory?
The way you missed the scientific jackpot
Was by so often sounding like a crackpot.

XC

Bombard atomic-number ninety-two,
And numbers ninety-three and ninety-four
Should be produced; and though they would be new,
They were seen coming—and what is more,
The current of events became so clear,
Two labs predicted them, and even claimed,
Quite independently, that 'twould appear,
Since ninety-two for Uranus was named,
That ninety-three should bring Neptune to mind;
And ninety-four should Pluto celebrate.
What would be found, e'en names to be assigned:
The tight'ning stream turned freedom into fate!
Or is it that the banks are never far;
We're just too blind to see how near they are?

XCI

(To Edwin McMillan)

Oh quiet genius, with such a thirst
To hike alone in deserts: honors rained
Down on your head, not least because you burst
The cap beneath which matter'd seemed contained.
With Veksler, but quite independently,
You co-discovered "phase stability";
And that this showed its time had surely come
Your Russian friend and you came to agree.
And though you had helped build the atom bomb,
You grew to hate the subsequent arms race;
And looked up from your orchids, with aplomb,
To call the thing a national disgrace.
Pipe-smoking family man and man of peace,
Your T-bird blew away the Queen of Greece!

XCII

(To Philip Abelson)

The mass of high-grade papers that you wrote;
Your many medals—Were many gold?
One can't but note you were a man of note;
Did abler son a father e'er behold?
And with McMillan you were first to make
A transuranic element. And who
Would quibble with its being the namesake
Of Neptune, taking from Klaproth a cue?
"Enough of pessimism," you temporized;
And maybe this was why, though you were forming
Some eco-friendly views, you minimized
The gath'ring evidence of global warming.
And so, while pessimism can paralyze,
Let's not let optimism anesthetize!

XCIII

To make things that are new seems not the same
As finding things that were already there;
"Invention" for the former is the name
To which "discovery" we can compare.
So Uranus was not by Herschel made,
But only found; the telescope he used
Invented was, which will not be gainsaid.
How could so clear a contrast be confused?
And yet plutonium was clearly *found*
By one Glenn Seaborg's having *made* the stuff;
And other elements thus shake the ground
Beneath a contrast that seemed firm enough.
And even Uranus: Was it *to us*
Not new? Discov'ry thus creates, we see;
And ev'ry new thing causing such a fuss
Discovers a potentiality.
So new things with the past have much to do;
And old things are, by being found, made new!

XCIV

I'd think the Sun would be ashamed to shine,
Unless he be indeed a brazen fellow;
My lover's deep brown eyes, so rich, so fine,
Make bare monotony of glaring yellow.
No less ashamed should be the Moon by night,
So dull she is, with light not e'en her own;
When dance my lover's eyes with inner light,
The pallid Moon is hopelessly outshone.
The stars as well may wish to disappear,
Lest we their far, cold, scattered light should see
'Longside my lover's eyes, so warm, so near,
And cent'ring (strange to say!) betimes on me.
Yet heav'nly lights, brought low: now may you rise,
For raising to my mind my lover's eyes!

XCV

The Titans had to th' underworld been banned;
But then against the gods *new* giants rose.
Each had a hundred arms, each arm, a hand;
And fire belching from the mouth and nose!
But even these the gods did soon subdue,
And 'neath Mount Etna bury them alive;
And when that mount erupts in molten spew,
'Tis that these giants for their freedom strive.
Their monstrous fall had made the island quake
Enough to stir the underworld's dark lord;
Black horses drew his chariot up to take
A look at what might need to be restored,
Lest his domain should somehow be laid bare
To th' upper world's unsympathetic stare.

XCVI

A lovely lake, embowered by the trees,
In the fair vale of Enna softly lies,
Where skin is e'er caressed by gentle breeze,
And violets and lilies kiss the eyes.
And dancing, singing, piping nymphs play here,
Their gentle music playing on the air;
So everything's as if arranged to cheer:
A world where nothing hints of worldly care.
'Twas here Proserpina, so fair to see,
One day had filled her basket up with flowers,
And then her apron too. Yet lingered she;
So peacefully she whiled away the hours!
In harmony with wood nymphs she would sing,
In Enna's valley of eternal spring.

XCVII

(Venus Fuming)

Minerva thinks herself too wise for love,
As if she had a brain but not a heart;
She thinks her thinking raises her above
The common god, who's not uncommon smart.
Then there's Diana: hunting fills her day.
She stalks and stalks, and takes her deadly aim
At *animals*! Ye gods, ungodly prey!
For them she scorns my vastly nobler game?
Proserpina? Too fair, her mother thinks,
For mating, when 'tis Ceres' vanity
Which matchless is! Since when is love a jinx?
WHO DO THEY THINK THEY ARE, DEFYING *ME*?
While in the very *bowels* of Earth is lurking
That filthy Pluto, at my empire *smirking*!

XCVIII

And as Proserpina in Enna's vale
Picked flowers, Pluto's iron chariot sped,
Drawn by his coursers black along the trail.
And well-marked was their course, and where it led;
For from Mount Eryx Venus all could see,
Where she sat watching her son Cupid play.
Not one to miss an opportunity,
She took him in her arms to sweetly say,
"My son, there is a growing disrespect
Among the gods for our whole enterprise;
Now is the time for action to correct
This nasty problem ere it multiplies.
"The dark lord is abroad! Go, plant a dart
Deep into Pluto's dirty, twisted heart!"

IC

Look there! What moving shadow do we see
Among long shadows on this wooded rise?
All else is still—Right there! What can it be,
Here in these hills below which Enna lies?
'Tis Cupid! for the archer has been sent
On mission bold by Venus, his mad mother;
And on success he's like his bow, well bent:
There crouches he, for he can do no other.
While in the shadows of late afternoon,
Proserpina, down in the vale below,
Her apron full of flowers, thinks that soon
With floral treasures she must homeward go.
Then Cupid, hearing hoofbeats, takes his station;
He draws his bow…his heart pounds… Thunderation!

C

Above the vale of Enna, Pluto drove
His four black stallions briskly on their way;
Down in the pleasant valley 'neath this grove
Was where he hoped to watch the close of day.
Though tremulous the monsters' recent fall,
Earth's crust, it seemed, retained integrity;
His underworld (all that he loved at all)
Seemed safe, and so he smiled contentedly.
But ere he leaves the grove, we hear him gasp,
Convulsed by pain now shooting through his chest!
His twitching hands at rounded handrail grasp!
He falls! In fetal curl he comes to rest.
His team gives harness bells a puzzled shake,
And draws up in a meadow by a lake.

CI

Had passers-by been on the scene to see
Poor Pluto in his chariot that day,
They may have thought him dead, so still was he,
Curled in the iron womb in which he lay,
A little like a babe already dead
In utero, so never to be tried
By life, a babe whose words would go unsaid
Forever, laughs unlaughed and tears uncried.
But Pluto was a god, and gods don't die;
He woke to jingling bells, and grasped the rail,
And raising himself up, cast groggy eye
About, to get his bearings in the vale…
Then rose his soul to Heav'n from darkling Earth!
It was, if ever was, a second birth!

CII

Proserpina herself was standing there!
Proserpina, who was beyond all art!
Proserpina, who was beyond compare!
Proserpina, who filled his empty heart!
Bowled over, Pluto stood there gazing down
Upon her flawless form in fading light;
His eyes then locked with hers, so bright! So brown!
"I beg your pardon—Are you alright?"
And Pluto wondered if 'twas all a dream:
Cannot in dreams our fantasies acquire
The guise of truth? And how else could she seem
So truly sculpted by his own desire?
And mighty Pluto, now twice-smitten god,
Could manage no more than a dumbstruck nod.

CIII

"I hope you will not think me over bold;
It is my nature to be rather shy.
Yet somehow, something makes me hope to hold
You here a moment, 'neath this evening sky.
"I rarely get to talk with anyone:
My mother keeps me under lock and key,
Except for picking flowers in the sun,
Here in the safety of this pleasant lea.
"I do not wish to sound like one to whine,
But just how many flow'rs must one girl pick?
I guess, with nymphs and all, it all looks fine;
But frankly, my existence makes me sick!"
So gods, like people, spill their guts to strangers;
It feels so safe; and that's one of its dangers!

CIV

Encouragement enough was Pluto's nod:
"I think my mother loves me, and means well;
But wanting one's own life: Is that so odd?
She's making my whole life a living hell!"
And Pluto winced, and closed his eyes of gray
At this aspersion on his dark domain;
Proserpina observed, with some dismay,
Their owner was no stranger to grave pain.
Distractedly, she gently shook her head;
Profuse brown hair on perfect shoulder stirred;
"How fine your horses are," was all she said.
And then, with Pluto yet to speak a word,
Into his chariot she quickly stepped;
And pleading, "Take me with you," softly wept.

CV

Proserpina's head moved upon his chest,
And Pluto found his face lost in her hair;
And as their bodies 'gainst each other pressed,
He breathed the scent of yellow flowers there.
"I love you," Pluto murmured, "and my love
Is past all reason, and is past all rhyme;
'Tis such as dreams and myths are fashioned of;
And I must love you for the rest of time.
"But where is it that you and I should go?
I have to tell you: Hades is my home.
And though my heart no longer lies below,
There's this to think of, should we elsewhere roam:
Up here I don't amount to anything;
Down there we'd share a throne, for I am king!"

CVI

Proserpina, e'en to her own surprise,
Was disinclined to think the matter through,
But cried, with deepest, darkest, shining eyes,
"Forever shall I share your Hell with you!"
By nobl' emotion was he thus unmanned,
And Pluto's mouth went dry, his legs felt weak.
He wondered that the latter let him stand;
He wondered when the former'd let him speak.
Then in her eyes, a look of sudden fear,
And fairest of all faces went quite pale.
"'Tis late; my mother will come seek me here;
We must make haste from out this pleasant vale!"
In setting sun, the sky went all aflame
As Pluto roused his horses, each by name.

CVII

Not on white horse her rescuer had come,
But in a chariot four black horses drew;
Proserpina, no longer feeling glum,
High in the air her flower-basket threw.
"Farewell, damn flowers! I am through with thee!"
As sixteen hooves beat thunder on the ground,
The giddy couple laughed aloud in glee,
And petals fluttered softly all around.
So up from Enna's valley they were drawn;
The horses, homeward bound, picked up their pace.
Though great the distance, little time had gone,
It seemed, when they approached the sacred place:
The river Alph! When Pluto smote its bank
With his fell trident, into Hell they sank!

CVIII

Through vast and ancient chambers of the dead,
Along the river Alph the chariot ran;
'Cross countless ghastly chasms they onward sped,
Through black coal ridges measureless to man.
And Pluto felt at home, for 'twas his home;
But what is stranger, stranger far to tell:
Proserpina, a stranger in strange gloam,
Felt nonetheless somehow at home in Hell!
And at a castle tow'ring in the gloom,
The dark lord drew his horses to a stop.
The couple were transported to a room,
A quiet chamber very near the top;
And there their love did sweetly consummate,
And afterward, a pomegranate ate.

CIX

(*Apologia pro Fabula Sua*)

But now I fear some readers there must be
Whose criticism I cannot avoid;
For, knowing something of mythology,
They have been growing more and more annoyed.
So to my pretty song they will not dance,
And though (they say) they wish things otherwise,
To turn what happened into a *romance!*
'Tis to pervert, not just to bowdlerize!
I know they have most versions on their side;
I know old masters model it their way:
A grabbing god, a goddess terrified...
To all of which I have but this to say:
All are agreed that Cupid's aim was true;
And rape's a thing true love could never do.

CX

To find her daughter, Ceres stalked the Earth!
Each failure to find her fed her wrath;
As goddess of all growing things, and birth,
She soon was leaving desert in her path.
At length, she found a nymph who said she'd seen
Proserpina in Pluto's dark domain,
Appearing well, and living like a queen;
It looked, indeed, as if she shared his reign…
So Ceres then to Jupiter appealed,
And Jupiter could not but be concerned
By dying stock and desiccated field;
Could he stand by and watch the world be burned?
He would dispatch fleet Mercury, pell-mell,
To try to free Proserpina from Hell.

CXI

The Fates three sisters are who have command
Of destiny itself. These sisters three
Had given Jupiter to understand
One thing: Proserpina, to be set free,
Must have ingested *nothing* while below.
So he told Mercury, "If Pluto's bride
Has eaten, we're in trouble, for I know
'Tis something that the Fates will not abide."
So Mercury went down, and duly told
Poor Pluto just what Jupiter had said.
Poor Pluto! How in Hell was he to hold
His heart's true love? And long he scratched his head.
When nearly in despair that they were beaten,
He saw the light: that apple they had eaten!

CXII

When Jupiter heard Mercury's report,
He found himself quite squarely caught between
The Fates and Ceres; time was growing short
For Earth, which Ceres really seemed to mean
To make a desert, if to her her child
Was not restored. So to the Fates he said,
"Must the poor girl forever be exiled
For eating *half an apple* 'mong the dead?"
To angry Ceres then he said, "See here:
The Fates are most displeased. What would you say
To spending with your daughter *half* the year?"
And Jupiter thus deftly saved the day.
So parted lovers pay for our warm weather,
When Ceres paints the Earth in tones bucolic;
And when we're cold, we let them be together;
Let's wish the pair one hell of a good frolic!

CXIII

Why do these eyes see anything save you,
And why is not your voice all I can hear?
Is touching you not all these hands should do,
This nose but draw your scents when you are near?
These lips of mine, that yet need common fare:
Can thus they use most of their pow'r to taste,
When they have savored lips beyond compare?
Why go these senses to such senseless waste?
Did I commit some heinous sin or crime
In this life, or in some life long before,
For which my senses now are serving time
To even up some hidden cosmic score?
Then comes redemption most magnificent:
Those sweet sensations for which they are meant!

CXIV

I feared we'd hear but all too little now
Of good old Pluto, with the dwarves below
Your standard planets pushed; I wondered how
School children would their planets come to know.
"Matilda Visits Every Monday; Just
Stays Until Noon" would nicely do the trick;
That tacked-on "Period" well could bite the dust,
So much the better in young minds to stick.
Or this: "My Very Energetic Mother
Just Served Us Nachos" (not "Nine Pizzas"). But
National Geographic had another
Objective: rather than see the list cut
To eight, they would extend it to eleven,
Thus making room for dwarves in "planet" heaven!

CXV

(My Very Exciting Magic Carpet Just Sailed Under Nine Palace Elephants)

What is it that the children ought to learn?
Just where should be their education's focus?
Away from *hoc est corpus* let us turn,
And from all mind-befogging hocus-pocus!
The ABC's are good, then the three R's;
Of arts and sciences, before they're through,
A little bit, I hope; and maybe Mars
Is something they could something learn of too.
And not just Mars, but all those other balls
(Including ours) that orbit 'round our Sun.
So thank you, little Maryn of Great Falls,
Montana, for help making it more fun;
And palace elephants: as 'neath you sail
Our children, brush them gently with your tail!

CXVI

Since everything that's heavier than lead
Is breaking down to lead, it's hard to see
Why science has not come right out and said:
This heavier stuff *true* elements can't be.
Or since the rocky inner planets four,
Plus four gas giants make a group of eight,
Why science, when it could declare "No more,"
Would rather add dwarf "planets" to the slate.
Something there is that wants a bundle bound,
A package neatly wrapped, with ribbon tied;
And yet it seems that science would confound
This urge instead of see it satisfied,
As if insisting that the final word
Has not yet been, nor ever will be, heard.

CXVII

(The Flammarion Woodcut)

'Neath yellow sky lie fields and tree of green
On a flat Earth. And in that yellow sky
Are Sun and Moon and stars, easily seen;
And on or 'neath a dome all these things lie.
Beyond this world as it to us appears
Lies a blue realm of things that truly are,
Where planets roll, as in celestial spheres,
From which the dome seems 'ranged our eyes to bar.
And at the lower left, in scarlet gown,
A weary pilgrim, who at last has found
The very place at which the dome comes down
To meet the Earth, crawls weakly on the ground.
Yet head and hand break through, as if to bond
Forever with the majesty beyond!

CXVIII

I dare say those who listen seem quite free,
When Triton, son of Neptune, makes his sound,
To hear whate'er they like; yet trumpetry
Of gods by mortal fantasy is bound.
And no less bound was Amalthea's horn,
By which the baby Jupiter was fed
Whatever he desired, once he had torn
It somehow from its home on that goat's head.
(Camille Flammarion was first to note
That one of Neptune's moons would well be named
For Triton; also that the Jovian goat
By moon of Jupiter should be acclaimed.)
So horns of plenty are a mere illusion;
Unbounded bounty, a complete delusion.

CXIX

In Boston grew the cotton mills, and soon
The mills made fortunes; from the fortunes grew
The Boston Brahmin class. With silver spoon
In mouth were born the children of these few.
And of no small concern to this high class
Was seeing that its children's education
(At Harvard) would be anything but crass,
And altogether fitting to their station.
But cotton could not be forever king,
And newer industries were taking root
In other cities; Brahmins felt the sting
Of seeing such new centers past them shoot.
So as they sipped their tea on Beacon Hill,
They worried that their town was standing still.

CXX

"My Darling Percy," so his mother wrote
To Percival, her eldest, favorite son;
His father was accordingly remote,
A proper Brahmin sire, not much for fun.
At Harvard, Percy turned out to excel
In the humanities, and science too;
Then in the family business did quite well:
It seems there wasn't much he couldn't do.
But he was champing at the Brahmin bit;
He and his clever friends were wont to scoff
At its restraints. So rather than submit
To Brahmin bridal plans, he broke things off;
And strongly set on being his own man,
Set off on a long journey to Japan.

CXXI

Young Percy Lowell proved he surely could
Make money; but from business he soon fled
To travel, as a way to seek *the good*
Instead of goods, as he's said to have said.
Experiencing the places that one went
And learning something of how people live
Would be the *worthy* traveler's intent,
And insight into one's own life would give.
But though he wanted strongly not to see
The mere "outsides of things," we do not find
He shared new ways of life whole-heartedly;
His past was not so eas'ly left behind.
To anyone who otherwise assumes:
His Tokyo rental house had eighteen rooms!

CXXII

The Western world did not know very much
Of Asia, but this ignorance decreased
When orienting books appeared with such
Grand titles as *The Soul of the Far East*.
And Percy Lowell, author of *The Soul*,
Was witty, rich, and dashing, as if made,
If anybody was, to play the role
Of public author; so the role he played.
Four books (and articles and poetry)
He wrote within a span of but ten years.
'Tween flurries of intense activity
Was leisure with bipolar bach'lor peers;
Not always flying high, but flying solo,
They partied hard, and played a lot of polo.

CXXIII

Throughout the Cosmos, Herbert Spencer taught,
From simple to complex, things rise through stages;
Thus, other beings capable of thought
Should have evolved elsewhere down through the ages.
So when *canali* on Mars were announced
By Schiaparelli, it caused quite a stir;
Upon his lovely drawings many pounced,
From such designs designers to infer!
And spurred by this, and by a recent book
In which he found Flammarion agreeing,
Percy Lowell, for his own good look,
Combed all the Earth for what is called "good seeing."
Might life on Mars, and scientific glory,
Be sought from Arizona Territory?

CXXIV

I'm glad 'twas not the use of psychotropics
That A. E. Douglass urged; instead, his letter
To Percy was concerned with telescopics,
To wit: "The higher we can get the better."
Where Beale's men in 1855,
To fly the flag, had stripped a stately pine,
A town on the plateau was all athrive,
And Douglass found the "seeing" truly fine.
(But by the year of 1958,
The town along Route 66 was fighting
What no stargazing site could tolerate:
The light pollution caused by outdoor lighting.
As of Tiresias we may remark:
Deep things are seen most clearly in the dark.)

CXXV

The reading public's taste began to turn
To strident critics of modernity;
The rising orientalist was Hearn,
And Lowell went into astronomy.
To study both the planets and the stars,
He founded a brand new observatory;
Its focus sharpened soon to life on Mars—
A search that seemed to promise fame and glory.
But others could not see the things he saw;
And his beloved mother Katharine died;
And at his mind self-doubts began to gnaw;
And publication pressures multiplied...
At forty-two, work-strained, bereaved, abashed,
The system that was Percy Lowell crashed.

CXXVI

In blessed moments when I feel your smile
Shine down on me, I dare say there is none
So richly gifted with the gift of guile
As to persuade me you are not the Sun.
But when in darkness you are my sole light,
And but for you I feel I would as soon
Surrender as keep up the losing fight,
'Tis no less clear to me: you are the Moon.
Sun, Moon (or planet)—which of these three
A piece of matter is, a matter is
That matters greatly to astronomy;
And it can be but one, which takes no whiz
To see. But as a *poet*, I may say
You are my Moon by night, my Sun by day.

CXXVII

We like to think we're sensible enough
To trust our senses—to scrutinize
Two lines and pick the longer's not too tough;
The evidence is right before our eyes!
But Asch ran studies of conformity,
And showed that what the normal human being
Will see (or claim to see) will often be
Whatever peer-group members say *they're* seeing.
So when they peered into his telescope,
His rich, distinguished friends (both guys and gals),
Who knew he'd been depressed but now had hope,
Saw just as well as Percy his canals;
And far be it from me to speak for you,
But I think I'd have seen the damn things too.

CXXVIII

The farther from its sun a planet flies,
The later in its life it has to be,
As youthful ardor to senescence dries,
And passion cools to calm passivity.
And Earth we find now in her very prime
Of life; but Mars, as farther out, is past—
Or nearly past—her fertile age. The time
Draws near when high life there must breathe its last.
And what but *build canals* should beings do
To tap the icecaps they saw ever shrinking?
What other course for desp'rate creatures who
Could feel their kind into extinction sinking?
So Percy thought he saw, through desert night,
A world rage against its fading light.

CXXIX

The mind of H. G. Wells was set arace
By visions of a planet cool and drying,
And of strange creatures living in that place:
An ancient species dying, dying, dying.
Ere Earth had quickened life, Mars quickened them;
And they were great, and almost found a way
Her aging, if not to reverse, to stem;
And so look forward to a brighter day.
But no. And so in cylinders they hailed
Down on the surface of a planet blue;
And when, with searing heat-rays, they'd prevailed,
Our planet would be theirs. We would be through.
We were, to them, as inconvenient worms;
Yet they fell victim—to novel germs!

CXXX

Canali! Anyone with decent eyes
Accustomed to the use of telescopes
Need do no more than look to realize
How firmly based are Percy Lowell's hopes!
Canali! If they mere illusions be,
We'd like to know, from those who thus protest,
Why phantoms would prove easiest to see
At times when seeing's at its very best?
Canali! Down in Chile they appeared
So well that one could fancy that one heard
(Wrote David Todd, who's long for Lowell cheered)
The bats above the pampa shriek the word!
As mass approval Percy deftly curried,
Establishment astronomers got worried…

CXXXI

Now, no one said that Percy was a *fake*,
As by his work the public was astounded;
But public faith in science was at stake,
Because his claims did not appear well founded.
And so top people felt it would be best
To interrupt their studies of the stars;
Refocusing their giant eyes, they'd test
As best they could the Lowell work on Mars.
The Lick refractor measured three feet wide,
While Percy's at Mars Hill was only two;
At Yerkes, a *five*-foot reflector tried
To see what Percy seemed to think he knew.
And Percy's lines broke into strings of features
That did not look designed by thinking creatures.

CXXXII

But Percy said that making out detail
Was not like picking up far points of light;
Refracting telescopes of modest scale
His pursuit suited just exactly right.
And Percy said it took a special eye
A planet's surface features to discern
(And that he had it, and was not too shy
To say so, one is not surprised to learn);
And Percy said it took a certain air,
For not just any atmosphere would do;
And Flagstaff was, for this, beyond compare;
It was an aura one could see right through.
His scope, his eye, his air: these gave best seeing!
But not too many experts were agreeing.

CXXXIII

Th' observatory Percy Lowell "built"
Seemed like one of a rich man's passing toys;
But Percy gave it an immortal tilt
By hiring two hardworking Hoosier boys.
So even experts who had come to cite
Poor Percy's work on Mars as good for laughs
Could find but little fault, try as they might,
With C. O. Lampland's stellar photographs.
And it was V. M. Slipher's to reveal
(Regardless of what might be found on Mars)
That spiral galaxies are fast awheel,
And there is gas and dust between the stars.
And so, to some extent despite its founder,
The place's scientific name grew sounder.

CXXXIV

Now Percy was a man of grace and style,
Which for a scientist's a little funny;
His shopping trips for clothes could last awhile,
And Percival, remember, had the money.
I guess he thought one might as well just try
To look as smart and tasteful as one can;
I think that Percy was too bright a guy
To really think it's clothes that make the man—
Or woman, though here too he was no dunce.
Lace blouses he most fav'rably assessed:
"Nothing in which a woman is at once
So dressed and so bewitchingly undressed"!
So Percy had an eye for more than Mars,
And Percy liked fine wine and good cigars.

CXXXV

From faith and family Irva feared to stray,
So that relationship did not quite burgeon;
Then he let charming Edith get away,
In part because she was not quite a virgin.
Miss Erna chased him not quite hard enough:
His amorous response, in his own phrase,
Was "incomplete." ('Tis but of late there's stuff
To help an aging man with *that* malaise.)
Meanwhile, his secretary made long strife
With Constance Keith for Percy (and their war
Continued after Constance was his wife,
And even after Percy was no more).
But Percy loved work more than love or sex;
And his next work was finding "Planet X"!

CXXXVI

His work on Mars, poor Percy Lowell knew,
Seemed in the process of evaporation;
He knew he needed something new to do
To save his scientific reputation.
Since Uranus's orbit seemed not quite
Explained by Neptune, his observatory
Would seek a "Planet X," and he just might
Yet bask in something like Le Verrier's glory.
Though fruitless when poor Percy's race was through
("His greatest disappointment," one friend called it),
The search would have survived him; but untrue
His widow, *Constance*, proved: her lawsuit stalled it.
Let those who say there's nothing in a name
Deny the irony, but not the shame.

CXXXVII

Late in the nineteenth century, it seemed
That Uranus's orbit was not quite
Explained by Neptune, so some experts deemed
A planet *farther* out would set things right.
In Flagstaff, Lowell's young observatory
By 1910 faced scholarly rejection:
Canals-on-Mars now seemed a crackpot story,
So Lowell sought a sober new direction.
In public, Percy never did retract
His views on Mars; yet meanwhile he retrained
His eyes on "Planet X." In point of fact,
He did so in a way—for him—restrained.
But while the folks at Flagstaff nobly tried,
In 1916, Percy Lowell died.

CXXXVIII

For ten long years the Lowell Observatory
Suffered the all-but-incessant ravages
Of litigation. 'Tis a dismal story:
The fault was Percy's widow's—Constance Savage's.
Perhaps it might be said she was just needy;
But hearing what it was that she contested,
We find she seems unfaithful and, well, greedy.
For 'twas the money that had been bequested
By her late husband Percy so the work
He cared so deeply for could be extended.
She lost. But thanks to this most unkind quirk
Of fate, his Planet-X search was suspended.
And nothing makes me minded to remonstrance
Like contemplating Percy's widow, Constance.

CXXXIX

When Roger Putnam (Percy's sister's son)
The trusteeship of Lowell did assume,
He was quite keen—the bitter court case won—
To see his "Uncle Percy's" quest resume.
With lens by C. A. R. Lundin well ground,
A special scope (thirteen-inch) was begun;
It rode a novel mounting, smooth and sound,
Machined by Stanley Sykes helped by his son.
The master carpentry that crowned it all
Was E. C. Mills' superbly fashioned dome.
(These last three craftsmen all were pleased to call
Not only Lowell friend, but Flagstaff home.)
And I don't hold with those who'd minimize
How much on others *each* of us relies.

CXL

Up from the plains of Kansas went a lad
To Flagstaff, Arizona; in his eyes
Were stars indeed, so he was very glad
To take a job observing desert skies.
He sought, on spectrographs two weeks apart,
What looked, against the stars, like moving specks;
And just before his second year would start,
Told Slipher, "I have found your Planet X!"
'Twas 1930, in the very place
Where Percy Lowell'd hoped and believed he spied
Canals on Mars, and then tried to save face
By finding "Planet X," and how he'd tried!
He'd failed, and failing, failed to still the jeers;
But still they were for him when rang the cheers
Of a whole planet in Clyde Tombaugh's ears,
For Percy had been dead for fourteen years.

CXLI

And when the institution she had tried
To plunder made a great discovery,
Did Constance shyly hesitate to guide
It as to what the latter's name should be?
Of course not! She said "Zeus" should be its name;
Then she said "Lowell" really would be best;
And finally (overcoming native shame),
Suggested "Constance," where she let things rest.
"It was a touchy situation," wrote
Clyde Tombaugh; but these names were quite rejected;
And when the staff were called upon to vote,
Unanimously "Pluto" was selected.
And since its first two letters are "PL,"
Their find honored their founder very well.

CXLII

Now when the staff at Lowell picked the name
Of "Pluto," it was from a list of three;
And though the losers seem a little lame,
They'd suited Putnam, Lowell's fine trustee.
"Minerva" would have helped with gender balance,
But had in fact already been employed
(Beneath its station, given the great talents
Of Wisdom's goddess) on an asteroid.
Put forth by one T. J. J. See was "Cronus";
But See, at Lowell some thirty years before,
Had quickly made his very name an onus
As prima donna hard not to abhor.
(I fear to See there was no "seeing" dearer
Than See by shining See in See's own mirror.)

CXLIII

(To Venetia Burney Phair)

I like to think he often read the news
At breakfast, and would read aloud if he
Had found an item he thought might amuse
The rest of you, but *you* especially.
I like to think that morning much the same
As others, when you heard your grandpa say—
To bait you?—that he wondered what they'd name
A whole new world found half a world away.
Though but eleven, you were rather keen
On Greco-Roman myth; and thus inspired,
And with no inkling of what it would mean,
"Why don't they call it Pluto?" you inquired.
And thus the pow'r of ancient lore and fable
Was conjured 'round the Burney breakfast table.

CXLIV

Falconer Madan, closing in on eighty,
Would make a most renowned octogenarian.
In English learned circles he was weighty:
Retired Oxford Bodleian's Librarian.
When to his friend at the observatory,
Its eminent director, H. H. Turner,
He told his touching Burney-breakfast story,
It found a most enthusiastic learner.
To Flagstaff Turner put the story through,
Where, backed up by the Madan-Turner combo,
Venetia's entry (too good to be new)
Was picked to name the thing found by Clyde Tombaugh.
Sometimes the question isn't "Who first said it?"
But "Whom would we most like to see get credit?"

CXLV

In Italy, at Brera, they'd confirmed
Clyde Tombaugh's sighting; and Geoff Nunberg notes
That Pluto's what the object had been termed
There ere the folks at Flagstaff cast their votes.
Moreover (and as Nunberg's also shown),
The name had been in use by H. M. Pickering,
A long-time Lowell rival too well known
To Slipher for his not infrequent bickering.
So 'twas Venetia's story, not her name
That resurrected Pluto from the dead.
But what of that? Would someone care to claim
Proserpina or Pluto could instead
Have done it? Hah! Let god or goddess try
To better write a name across the sky!

CXLVI

Not for a Disney dog, as sometimes fabled,
Was Pluto designated; that was done
In 1930, while the dog was labeled
With that tag not 'til 1931.
The only way to be *named after* something
Is for the something to have come before;
Since thinking otherwise would be a dumb thing,
I don't imagine I would say much more
Had not Venetia Phair (and others) said
That things were just the other way around.
And this may be, but I confess I'm led
To think there's something more we've not yet found,
For why would Walt have thought a dog named after
A planet (or a god) would cause much laughter?

CXLVII

I'm told there lies deep in the favored land
Of southern Indiana a small town
They call French Lick; and I can understand
That there the pace of modern life slows down
So soothingly that many recreate
Themselves by going there, where they resort
The wooded hoosier hills to contemplate,
If not at golf or tennis to disport.
And also there, surrounded by a moat,
A large hotel casino will amuse
The guests; but though it's shaped like riverboat,
What they'll be taken for is not a cruise!
Against the house, the luckiest of choosers
At length, if not yet beggars, will be losers.

CXLVIII

I hope the reader does not labor under
The false impression I've strayed from my story;
If so, I hasten to correct my blunder
By telling you of French Lick's greatest glory.
For there, up from below the ground, there bubbles
A water blessed with the noteworthy power
To cure the uptight guests of certain troubles
Internally within a single hour.
They bottled it, red devil on the label;
It had a slogan reassuring still,
Which, owing to research, I now am able
To share: "When Nature Won't, PLUTO Will."
As of old-fashioned ketchup in a bottle
'Twas said, "First none'll come, and then a lot'll."

CIL

For Pluto Water's what they called the stuff;
And rich with min'rals from beneath the ground,
It scarcely can be said strongly enough:
The name and symbol were no less than sound.
So marketed, the product met success.
For untold millions who were prone to ailing
From constipation's ever-pressing stress
It must have made for rather smoother sailing.
By 1930, it was so well known
For its capacity to cleanse the gut
That anything named "Pluto" would be prone,
'Twas feared, of anal jokes to be the butt.
Would Pluto's name thus languish here below?
Of course not! That's at least one thing we know!

CL

"Mamma slapped me!" Wiping at his eyes,
The little boy embodies desolation;
And reading on, the lad, we realize,
Is victim of his mother's constipation.
And to the boy what do we see extend
Consoling paw? A *dog*. Whatever got 'er
So mad, his mom, to mellow, need but spend
A modest sum to buy some Pluto Water!
With or without this ad, I can't but think
(At times, loose ends are what need tying up)
The laxative connection is the link
That made "Pluto" a droll name for a pup.
Timewise, this ad (in *Liberty*) seems fine:
October 19, 1929.

CLI

Lest it be thought I'm building up a tissue
Of outright lies or idle speculations:
We *know* that Pluto Water was an issue,
Because we have on record reservations
Expressed by R. L. Putnam, sole trustee
Of Lowell Observatory, in a letter
To its Director Slipher, who could see
The problem, but thought they could do no better.
French Lick, beyond the shadow of a doubt,
Had loosed the bowels of an entire nation
(Casino ne'er could better clean one out!);
Is that a wholly foul association?
And so, to Slipher, sulfur water's stink,
Like love and fame, to nothingness did sink.

CLII

"When Nature Won't, PLUTO Will"? A nit
I hope is not what I'm about to pick
O'er this old slogan, which helped make a hit
Of sulfur water shipped out from French Lick.
The springs themselves seem *natural* enough,
And does not *Nature* bid us all to drink?
And what emerges once we drink the stuff,
Is wholly *natural*, I can't but think.
Now, that the water had to be discovered
And named by us are facts I won't deny;
But aliens who high above us hovered
And studied us awhile would wonder why
Discovering and naming things should be
Split off from *natural* causality.

CLIII

Along with sugar, salt's the sort of thing
Of which we like to eat more than we should.
This said, I guess it's time I took a fling
At something some have said they wish I would.
Now, evolution seems to tell us why
We'd want too much of good things of this kind:
Long ages past of chronic short supply
Would favor wanting all that we could find.
Near where the *French* had built a fort, the springs
Left salt deposits creatures came to *lick*.
Such tasty sites, called licks, are special things;
So to this place "French Lick" soon came to stick.
Are saltier things suggested by the name,
Which go beyond a certain kind of kiss?
Though steamy poetry is not my game,
This chance for a love sonnet I'll not miss;
But be forewarned that neither there you'll see
A single word of gross anatomy.

CLIV

Oh absent-minded kiss! Is couple found,
That's coupled been more than a little while,
That does not know your feckless little sound,
Or recognize your distant, vacant smile?
You're prone to strike, or so it seems to me,
When starts or ends the ordinary day;
And so, to many, habit seems to be
A hungry worm that eats true love away.
And yet sweet ways there be that lovers find,
And travel o'er and o'er but cannot name;
They leave what's ordinary far behind,
By same old roads that seem not twice the same.
I swear by all below and all above:
No sweeter habits are than those of love!

CLV

Assuming Pluto to have been quite large
(Before it turned out to be far too small
For "Planet X"), G. Kuiper thought the marge
Beyond held nothing—nothing at all.
A theory of our system's edge worth more,
As time would tell, proposed that past Neptune
A ring of icy matter held in store
More "Plutos" that would be discovered soon
Or late; and since of late they have, I've felt
That Kenneth Edgeworth might be more acclaimed.
Though one may see the "Edgeworth-Kuiper Belt,"
It's mostly "Kuiper Belt": a structure named
(And this must be more than a little rare)
For someone who believed it wasn't there.

CLVI

If a mere golf ball represents the Sun
At Yankee Stadium's home plate, we know
A trip to Neptune would take a home run;
And the next star would be in Chicago!
Such is the size and emptiness of space.
In search of something solid, shall we turn
To matter? Well, supposing we replace
Our Sun with golf-ball nucleus, we learn
That centered, its electrons, far afield,
Would haunt the stadium's remote recesses.
The Cosmos thus appears to stand revealed
As but the union of two emptinesses!
I think Democritus might feel annoyed
To hear how filled the atoms are with void.

CLVII

Chicago's where their friends thought they would wed,
But Glenn and Helen from the train stepped down
Far from the madding crowd, en route, instead
Into the very small Nevada town
Of Caliente, which, good as its name,
Was hot indeed; and dust was all around.
But as for marriage, the couple's aim:
No one to make it legal could be found!
But Pioche, twenty-five miles up the road
(At length a local man named Ev advised),
Could boast a judge, so with the mailtruck's load
They got delivered, and were legalized
As soon as Helen Griggs had watched her guy,
Glenn Seaborg, polish off his apple pie.

CLVIII

An element was found, that much was clear;
And though, like the whole world, it was unstable,
When wartime secrecy should disappear
It would extend the periodic table.
The underworld's dark lord, 'twas clear as well,
Should figure in the name of this new thing;
While "plutium" caused Glenn's ear to rebel,
"Plutonium" had an attractive ring.
"Pl" (a lot like Pluto's), 'tis well said,
Is what its symbol really should have been;
But Seaborg wrote "Pu" ('Pee-yoo!') instead!
(Did Pluto Water prompt the nerdy sin?)
And thus the star-crossed mark of Percy Lowell
No more on chart than *planet* boasts bestowal.

CLIX

(To Glenn Seaborg)

We had to have the bomb you helped create
Because its awesome power to destroy
Was one the Nazis would not hesitate,
If able, against humans to deploy.
And with six colleagues, in the Franck Report,
You urged the world be shown what it could do
To desert or bare isle ere we resort
To targeting a populous milieu.
If Harry Truman ever even heard
Your message, it was one he did not heed;
And not your test, the one that soon occurred,
But still a most instructive "test" indeed,
Which made our new and awful peril plain;
And few, we hope, have fallen less in vain.

CLX

(To Grace Mary Coryell)

'Twas not to Mount Olympus that they went,
Your husband and the others such as he;
To Oak Ridge by their nation were they sent,
To learn deep secrets deep in secrecy.
They freed the energy in atoms bound!
When in the ashes of uranic fission
An element long sought they finally found,
You named it after a disturbing vision
That placed the scientists in bold compare
To rash Prometheus, who 'gainst all odds,
So humankind their awful power might share,
Had dared to steal fire from the gods.
Grace Mary! These new Titans you arraigned:
To what dread Caucasus would *they* be chained?

CLXI

If so offended, why are they still here?
Just when and why they came we do not know;
But served they are—and were, from love or fear,
Since their obscure arrival long ago.
As guests, the gods have been remarkably
And also variously inclined to tell
Their hosts how to behave: now lovingly,
Now ruthlessly, to slay the infidel.
Yet with our very flesh and blood we've wined
And dined them decently, and rather more;
So it would scarcely seem rude or unkind
Were we to now escort them to the door.
Their long and storied stay is all but through;
Come, let us bid the deities adieu!

CLXII

Two million and well more was the estate
That Percy'd left, and though he'd made provision
Quite gen'rously for his surviving mate,
That she should have it *all* was *her* decision.
She'd tried to break his will, and she was beaten;
But by that time, in 1925,
Well over half the estate had been eaten
Away by legal costs; barely alive
Was the observatory. I have read:
Those who love money won't be satisfied
With money. And the Reverend Gemmell said
In '54, when Constance finally died,
This "benign witch," who'd lived so for the dollar,
Came to her lonely end in "opulent squalor."

CLXIII

Discoverer of Pluto in his youth,
Clyde Tombaugh ended a nonagenarian;
By no means faithless, his long search for truth,
For Clyde had been a faithful Unitarian.
And I have heard him called the most respected
Astronomer—faint praise, some may propose—
To rank with folks who claim to have detected
Those objects fondly known as UFO's.
But Clyde was softer in the heart than head,
To judge by widow Patsy's true devotion;
"He was a *scientist*," she firmly said,
And would have understood Pluto's demotion.
And most of th' astroids Clyde found in his life
He kindly named for grandkids, kids, and wife.

CLXIV

Not far from the Grand Canyon is the place
Where Percy long peered into the abyss
And thought he saw, across the martian face,
Canals. And I think I would be remiss
Did I not mention that it's pretty clear:
The water 'neath the surface there is bound
As ice, and in no way does it appear
That martians or canals are to be found.
But I suggest we take a little care,
For others and ourselves as well as Mars,
To tend more to what is than is not there:
Huge craters and volcanoes, gaping scars
Like *Valles Marineris*, which could hold
Our own Grand Canyon half a thousandfold.

CLXV

So Mars is not the wonder Percy hoped,
And Pluto's not the kind of thing we thought;
And lately the astronomers have coped
With those of Pluto's fans who seemed distraught
By offering "plutoid" to name the kind
Of thing that Pluto is. Now, though some took
This as a slight, I'm of a different mind.
To put the matter plainly: in my book,
To name a *kind* of thing's a higher thing
Than just to name a thing; PLutoids may glide
Around a billion systems! The dark king
Bears Percy on a cosmic chariot ride!
Farewell. I bid you think with joy, not woe,
Of god, and erstwhile planet, named Pluto.

FINIS

Index of First Lines

Above the vale of Enna, Pluto drove, 106
A fine and comely couple, it appears, 68
A global body called the I. A. U., 79
A half a dozen times ere he was through, 49
Along with sugar, salt's the sort of thing, 159
A lovely lake, embowered by the trees, 102
And as Proserpina in Enna's vale, 104
And when the institution she had tried, 147
An element was found, that much was clear, 164
A pebble: it is difficult to name, 44
Assuming Pluto to have been quite large, 161
Astronomy in France had sunk quite low, 90
At the outset, did God, who all things knew, 19
A Universe of atoms in the void, 65
Ben Franklin's bastard was to be your groom, 54
Bombard atomic-number ninety-two, 96
Bright gem of the Aegean! Who will dare, 7
But now I fear some readers there must be, 115
But Percy said that making out detail, 138
By naming the new planet for his king, 53
Canali! Anyone with decent eyes, 136
Cassini, brains like yours one seldom sees, 43
Chicago's where their friends thought they would wed, 163
Coordinates are a good way to show, 50
Could God have made the orbits less than round, 24
Did not what we call Earth go 'round the Sun, 16
Discoverer of Pluto in his youth, 169
Earth, water, air, and fire: each had its home, 63
Encouragement enough was Pluto's nod, 110
Falconer Madan, closing in on eighty, 150
For Epicurus Descartes had no time, 27
For gods the Romans named the wand'ring stars, 10
For Pluto Water's what they called the stuff, 155
For ten long years the Lowell Observatory, 144
From Descartes' *cogito* we know he found, 26

From faith and family Irva feared to stray, 141
From soldiering you turned to alchemy, 41
Had passers-by been on the scene to see, 107
His work on Mars, poor Percy Lowell knew, 142
How many planets should we say there are, 82
How stupid could you be? Enough to fight, 22
I dare say those who listen seem quite free, 124
I'd think the Sun would be ashamed to shine, 100
If a mere golf ball represents the Sun, 162
I feared we'd hear but all too little now, 120
If parts, well weighed, still weigh less than a whole, 72
If so offended, why are they still here, 167
If we decide we want stability, 76
I hope the reader does not labor under, 154
"I hope you will not think me over bold," 109
I like to think he often read the news, 149
Imaginer of worlds, you claimed this world, 36
I'm glad 'twas not the use of psychotropics, 130
I'm told there lies deep in the favored land, 153
In blessed moments when I feel your smile, 132
In Boston grew the cotton mills, and soon, 125
In France was quick Cassini quick to find, 42
In Italy, at Brera, they'd confirmed, 151
In the beginning God made heaven and Earth, 17
John Dalton saw that simple ratios, 80
Late in the nineteenth century, it seemed, 143
Lest it be thought I'm building up a tissue, 157
Le Verrier told the Germans where to aim, 91
Look, look before you leap! Let us not doubt, 70
Look there! What moving shadow do we see, 105
Lucretius indeed in very Rome, 8
"Mamma slapped me!" Wiping at his eyes, 156
Mapmaker, we know nothing of your looks, 14
Minerva thinks herself too wise for love, 103
"My Darling Percy," so his mother wrote, 126
My love is lover of a planet blue, 93
'Neath yellow sky lie fields and tree of green, 123
Not far from the Grand Canyon is the place, 170
Not for a Disney dog, as sometimes fabled, 152
"Nothing exists but atoms and the void," 9
Not on white horse her rescuer had come, 113
Now droops the raven slouched upon a skull, 12

Now, no one said that Percy was a *fake*, 137
Now Percy was a man of grace and style, 140
Now to my winter comes a discontent, 94
Now when the staff at Lowell picked the name, 148
Of just exactly what do things consist, 62
Oh absent-minded kiss! Is couple found, 160
Oh country boy, how did it come to pass, 85
Oh quiet genius, with such a thirst, 97
O Marduk (Jupiter), 'tis in your grip, 13
One autumn day in 1845, 88
One of ten children born to German Jew, 51
One of your eyelids drooped, as if to wink, 57
Proserpina, e'en to her own surprise, 112
Proserpina herself was standing there, 108
Proserpina's head moved upon his chest, 111
Pythagoras five perfect solids knew, 23
Since everything that's heavier than lead, 74
Since everything that's heavier than lead, 122
Sir William Herschel had a son named John, 67
Six planets and six moons: a package neat, 40
So just why is there anything at all, 25
So Mars is not the wonder Percy hoped, 171
Some elements for planets have been named, 78
So what's your sign? Aquarius you say, 15
Strange, quiet low-born boy: Who knew your pain, 87
"That star's not on the map!" a young man cried, 86
The area of a rectangle is base, 45
The atoms of a single isotope, 83
The center of the Hunter's blade's not keen, 37
The composition of the crust of Earth, 73
The cycle of light and dark defines our days, 11
The elements are numbered by their Z's, 75
"The elements, they number 92," 81
The farther from its sun a planet flies, 134
The Fates three sisters are who have command, 117
The gap from Mars to Jupiter should hold, 64
The Goldilocks Zone! Not too hot or cold, 38
The ground beneath our feet, it seems to me, 71
The heavens would not long enroll the fame, 56
The mass of high-grade papers that you wrote, 98
The mind of H. G. Wells was set arace, 135
The moving object William Herschel found, 52

The reading public's taste began to turn, 131
The sky god, born of Earth, engorged her womb, 47
The thought has suddenly occurred to me, 77
The Titans had to th' underworld been banned, 101
The Western world did not know very much, 128
They say four hundred telescopes were "built," 59
They say your brewer father could not see, 48
They seem to most of us less than your art, 95
Th' observatory Percy Lowell "built," 139
Throughout the Cosmos, Herbert Spencer taught, 129
Through vast and ancient chambers of the dead, 114
To find her daughter, Ceres stalked the Earth, 116
To glorify his famous patrons' name, 30
To hide her from wife Juno's prying eyes, 31
To hunt a planet you were far from keen, 89
To make things that are new seems not the same, 99
To reach the very top! Some have to try, 69
'Twas not to Mount Olympus that they went, 166
Twelve meters long was Herschel's largest scope, 58
Two million and well more was the estate, 168
Unpopular beliefs o'erflow your mind, 21
Up from the plains of Kansas went a lad, 146
Vincenzo Galilei played the lute, 28
Was Evil made by Adam and by Eve, 18
Was Galileo bright and handy too, 29
Was it with gladness or with some regret, 32
We had to have the bomb you helped create, 165
We like to think we're sensible enough, 133
What is it that the children ought to learn, 121
What's harder to believe than that Earth moves, 20
When a new planet came within his scope, 61
When barriers to our love filled my poor head, 46
When Bruno had been tried for heresy, 34
When Jupiter heard Mercury's report, 118
"When Nature Won't, PLUTO Will"? A nit, 158
When Roger Putnam (Percy's sister's son), 145
When thanks to Jove the giants' time was through, 84
When you told Anna you'd take your own life, 66
Whether the optic's piercing eyes, 55
Why do these eyes see anything save you, 119
With astronomical egg on their face, 92
With Earth no more the point of reference, 39

You must have been the apple of his eye, 35
Young Percy Lowell proved he surely could, 127
You were eleven years younger than he, 60
You with your live-in lover children had, 33